THE ATHEIST WORE GOAT SILK

THE ATHEIST WORE GOAT SILK

POEMS

Anna Journey (signature)

~~ANNA JOURNEY~~

For Lucie —
With deepest admiration
and gratitude for your poetry.
Your fan,

Anna

LOUISIANA STATE UNIVERSITY PRESS
BATON ROUGE

Jan. 25, 2017

Published by Louisiana State University Press
Copyright © 2017 by Louisiana State University Press
All rights reserved
Manufactured in the United States of America
First printing

Designer: Laura Roubique Gleason
Typeface: Adobe Garamond Pro
Printer and binder: LSI

Library of Congress Cataloging-in-Publication Data
Names: Journey, Anna, 1980– author.
Title: The atheist wore goat silk : poems / Anna Journey.
Description: Baton Rouge : Louisiana State University Press, [2017]
Identifiers: LCCN 2016027489 | ISBN 978-0-8071-6568-3 (pbk. : alk. paper) | ISBN 978-0-
    8071-6569-0 (pdf) | ISBN 978-0-8071-6570-6 (epub) | ISBN 978-0-8071-6571-3 (mobi)
Classification: LCC PS3610.O6794 A6 2017 | DDC 811/.6—dc23
LC record available at https://lccn.loc.gov/2016027489

The paper in this book meets the guidelines for permanence and durability
of the Committee on Production Guidelines for Book Longevity of the
Council on Library Resources. ∞

for Alicia Jones

CONTENTS

ACKNOWLEDGEMENTS

Grateful acknowledgment is made to the editors and staff of the following publications in which these poems first appeared: Academy of American Poets' *Poem-a-Day:* "Accidental Blues Voice," "The Atheist Wore Goat Silk," and "Mississippi: Origins"; *AGNI:* "Habitual"; *The Atlas Review:* "Omens I Chose to Ignore"; *Blackbird:* "A Wayward Cow's Worst Nightmare," "Biosentimentality," and "One Year after My Move to California, I Jell-O Wrestle My Texan Past in a Dream"; *Columbia: A Journal of Literature and Art:* "Fried Chicken Prom Corsage (2): *Danse Macabre*" and "To Stop Tears while Chopping an Onion, Hang a Slice of Bread out of Your Mouth"; *diode:* "Blue Honey"; *FIELD:* "Asymmetrical—," "Fried Chicken Prom Corsage: Ode to My Thirties," "I Have a Problem with the Erotic History of Musk," and "Reasons Why Licking the Anesthetic Backs of Waxy Monkey Tree Frogs Could've Made Me Stand Living in Texas"; *Great River Review:* "In the Categories of Smells, Pears Are Considered Ethereal," "The Dildophone," "Middle School Sleepover: Jessica Accidentally Steps on My Right Eye," and "Rapture"; *The Journal:* "*Trompe-l'œil* for Shannon" and "*Welcome, Stranger*"; *Kenyon Review Online:* "Blues for the Semiaquatic," "I Find a Photograph Online of a Taxidermied Fox Posed in Front of a Flaming Grey Paisley Couch Abandoned in a Field of Crabgrass," and "Last Nostalgia Starting with a Piece of Spider Plant on Our Car's Backseat"; *Narrative:* "Upon Asking the Cashier at Kroger to Scan That Old Tattoo of a Barcode on My Forearm"; *New South:* "Nocturnal Activity"; *Parnassus:* "Foxing"; *Prairie Schooner:* "Bloodlines," "*Eat Shit, Martine:* Prescription for a Southern Belle," "Last Barbecue," and "Swan Fingers"; *The Southern Review:* "Accidental Theft: Crazy Quilt," "As a Child, My Mother Took a Girl Scout Field Trip to the Men's Ward of a New Orleans Prison," "I Sip an Herbal Tea Called *Gypsy Cold Care*," "My Grandparents' Siamese Cat, Sheba, Brain Damaged from a Crochet Hook," "Past Life Evaporation Riff," "Reminder to My Past Self in Which I Employ the Scientific Term *Drunken Forest*,"

"To the Peeping Tom Who Disguised Himself as an Oklahoma Night," and "Visiting Richmond after Several Years Away, I Discover a Restaurant Called L'Opossum"; *Third Coast:* "Our Weeklong Stay in the Magnolia Hotel that Started with a Mermaid Skeleton: Hurricane Evacuation, Austin"; *Tin House:* "Summer of Choosing the Dress" and "Victorian Chamber Pot My Mother Used as a Planter for Climbing Ivy."

I owe the zucchini-prank detail in the poem "Habitual" to Kate Ballantyne, who once told me a similar story.

Thanks to the folks at LSU Press: MaryKatherine Callaway, Jenny Keegan, Neal Novak, and Erin Rolfs. Gratitude to Jessica Faust and Emily Nemens of *The Southern Review.*

Thanks to my agent, Chris Clemans, of the Clegg Agency.

Gratitude to Sean Bishop for his editorial advice.

Thanks to Gülin Hayat Topdemir and Galeri Zilberman for graciously allowing me to use the painting *5 O'Clock Tea* on the cover of this book.

Love and gratitude to David St. John.

ONE

Upon Asking the Cashier at Kroger to Scan That Old Tattoo of a Barcode on My Forearm

Turns out my body's a dollar sweet potato
her register's screen said, as she lifted

her scanner, and I laughed. I can finally call myself
Garnet, Georgia Jet, Carolina Red. Those names

of tubers—my accidental totems. So many
varieties. I might slather

my arm in marshmallows, burrow
deep into the southern earth. I'd gotten

the tattoo at nineteen, drunk, after Alicia and I
sneaked into the Jefferson—the fanciest

hotel in Richmond with its old
Deco fountain in the lobby

where pet alligators swam circles
through the Jazz Age. We sat on velveteen

love seats wearing ripped jeans among the suits
of Virginia politicians and Baptist preachers,

daring each other: *I'll get a tattoo
if you do.* We discussed passion

vines on biceps or matching dragonflies
winging our asses. I swirled my plastic

flask's bourbon, decided we'd make
a statement about consumerism—blue

barcode stamped on each of our forearms.
After the hotel manager kicked us out,

for vagrancy, I tore a page from a book
of grocery store coupons so the tattoo artist

would have an image to copy: a barcode's
exact marks. I didn't think to stop

and choose which vegetable,
which object, didn't know my body

would soften beneath the lines. Ten years
later I'd finally ask a woman

to scan the ink, wondering why
I'd waited this long to find out

I've always been sweet but slightly
twisted, I've always been

waiting to disappear like this,
bite by bite, into someone's mouth.

Accidental Blues Voice

My ex-lover received it at seventeen
skiing the steep slope at Wintergreen called

Devil's Elbow. The early snowmelt along the Blue
Ridge had slipped the white limb of a birch

through the crust, jutted that camouflaged tip
into the center of the trail. He hit it, full speed,

flipped over his ski poles. One of them split
his vocal cords with its aluminum point. He sprawled

in the snow, his pink throat skewered like Saint
Sebastian or the raw quiver of his Greek father's

peppered lamb kebobs. The doctors didn't let him speak
for a year and when he finally tried his choirboy

voice had gravel in it. His tenor had a bloody
birch limb in it, had a knife in it, had a whole lower

octave clotted in it, had a wound and a wound's
cracked whisper in it. The first time I heard him

sing in his blues band, five years after the accident,
I told him his smoked rasp sounded

exactly like Tom Waits. Like my grandfather
sixty years since the iron lung. I couldn't believe

a growl like that crawled up from the lips
of a former Catholic schoolboy. But as he shut off

the halogen overhead—leaving only the ultraviolet
of his bedside's black light—he stroked my cheek,

crooned, *Goodnight, Irene.* His teeth and his throat's
three-inch scar glowed a green neon.

Fried Chicken Prom Corsage: Ode to My Thirties

It's when I sucked the velour
antler-buds of an adolescent

mule deer in a dream until my front teeth

broke off that I began
to take inventory. I'm tired

of trying to impress people. Heels

derange me. Red wine
won't let me sleep. No, I never did go

to my high school prom as a teenager. Lately,

I've noticed an ad for the "fried
chicken prom corsage"—a novelty object

sold by a florist in Kentucky. I suddenly

wished I'd had the chance to wear one. The golden-breaded
cluster of drumsticks cinched

in their fuchsia ribbons and a wrist-

elastic. That brutal
extravagance I had once. But, I must say, I look

better in this decade—toned

abs, no frizz, a manageable neurosis. I should throw
myself a party for having

even survived. The fried

chicken prom corsage could be
optional. The small legs

broken and crossed, hardened and tied.

Habitual

You knew my ritual of leaping nude

into the middle of our mattress each night
after switching

off the bedroom lights. I left
the ceiling fan on. I liked
the rush. I liked you

downstairs, slapping

some last notes
on your upright bass

in front of the brick fireplace. You knew

my habit of letting my patch
of zucchini in our backyard grow

monstrously obese—thick as thighs,
fibrous, leached

of flavor—the woody slices
only good

to mash for zucchini bread. You said
I had a green thumb

up my ass, that I made
the laziest gardener.

Which was true.

One night as a Halloween
prank you

waited until I turned on

the shower, picked the three
biggest zukes—longer

than baseball bats, lumpy, and watermelon-
fat. As I blasted

music from the bathroom
you slipped the bundle into bed,

tucked it in and fluffed
the down comforter so I wouldn't notice

the bumps. When I stepped
out of the shower, still

steaming, still mouthing

the words to the Stones' "Hot Stuff," I strutted
down the hall to our bedroom, shut off
all the lights. I leaped

onto the mattress, shrieked as the zucchini

began to cave and crack. The sound:
a pop like calcium

fracturing. I thought I'd snapped
the neck and arthritic
hind legs

of our sleeping cat. You watched the scene

crouched low
on the staircase as I tore

off the covers, exposed the boneyard

of broken zukes. When I finally
stopped shaking, I noticed

your face. Your grin flickered

beneath the handrail, framed
between banisters,
lit like that

jack-o'-lantern I could smash.

Bloodlines

My grandmother woke to find the right
side of the bed empty, the waft

of single malt throbbing
the hallway. She knew my grandfather

had once again crawled out
a first-story window to wander

their neighborhood while drunk.
He'd sunk toward the hard

lip of his highball glass every night
since his best friend from med school

shot himself. Bob called
from a swampside motel during the middle

of a dinner party my grandfather'd thrown
for his new psych residents—

the nude globes of Japanese
lanterns strung from the patio's

live oaks. When my grandfather called
back after his guests had left,

the motel's rotary phone rang
and rang through Bob's room, hours

after the shot. The cops called
my grandmother every few weeks

when they'd spot him
swaying in the streetlight, silver-bearded,

seemingly lost, muttering, *Hang on,*
Bob, just one last toast, as he turned

toward that champagne
cork's pop. The cops told her

the streets' coordinates
so she could drive in their Cadillac

to find him. The last Christmas
he was alive, my grandfather gave

my father a monogrammed copper
gumbo pot. I reached out

to rub his initials—engraved
and ground smooth. I'd do this again

at my grandfather's slot—
over his own name in the marble wall

of the chapel mausoleum. Each time
I visit my childhood home, I walk

through the hallway's fogged
portraits to the steaming kitchen,

where the pot's metal alloy
smells like blood filling the house.

To Stop Tears while Chopping an Onion, Hang a Slice of Bread out of Your Mouth

How have I wept all the way into my thirties
without knowing this? Christmas

Eve, my mother hands me a slice as we begin
to chop at the kitchen counter. She says,

Bite it to keep from crying. The bread's pocked texture
sucks up the vapors, stops the red onion's

acid from rising to my eyes. I could've used
this trick, each time I couldn't sleep

those years in Texas—the white oak swamp's
wafts of methane, the idling pickups, the *fuck yous*

I spat and left hanging in the air. The man
I left there. Or the flare of my dead

closeted grandfather—brandy cobbling
the bottom of his breath as he crawled out

of his ground-floor window for weeks
to wander the neighborhood after his lover's

suicide, drunk, muttering, still wearing
Bob's tweed hat. He'd leave my grandmother

asleep until the cop's phone call. The gossip
rose to follow him: the gay psychiatrist always

passed over for promotions, the madman
in his silver beard, barefoot near

the Jackson interstate. I'd replace
my tongue with a slice, hold onto that bite

long enough to swallow all the rising
toxins that would scald us, and keep them.

The Dildophone

Name of the instrument invented
by my ex-lover, who once played
string bass in a jug band—that silicone
dildo he'd rubber-banded by the flesh-
colored root to the narrow stem
of a yellow kitchen funnel. The funnel's
flared mouth formed the bell of a mock-
trombone, and the dildo dangled
below it, jutting out like a brass slide
or strap-on. He'd grab the shaft
and lift the small end of the funnel
to his lips, hum through it
like the tip of a kazoo. During gigs
he'd jump from behind his upright bass
to the stage's center, between
the banjo and mandolin players, red-
bearded and wiggling as he swung
the dildophone's cock. For a solo
he'd jack off the shaft as if to alter
the instrument's pitch. I'd sit
at a table in the middle of the bar, smile
as I sipped my beer. I liked to listen
for people who'd laugh and gasp: *Holy shit!*
Is that a dildo? The drunk audience
couldn't stop whooping. After the solo
someone always sent up a rum
and Coke. They didn't know
how his mother slapped him when,
at fifteen, he traded his violin
for an electric bass, or the way she'd pop
another codeine and make him—three
years old—balance a pencil against

the spruce body of a toy fiddle
for an hour each day so he could practice
holding a bow, even though
the faux instrument was stringless. His elbow
bent at the proper angle, his chin
tilted, his back straight. Sometimes
if she looked away, he'd start to hum
and feel the body resonate. Even
the pencil began to shake.

Foxing

—a term describing the sepia-colored spots on antique paper

Lately, the pages of my personal
library's books bristle
with an animal trace. It must be the way

the Texas humidity oxidized
the iron deep
in the paper's pulp, though I believe

it's the glimpse of a pelt
reappearing from
my childhood: that wild fox

gaunt between dogwoods. The one
I watched slip
its red thread

through the evening, sing something
vulpine to the neighbor's chained-
up chow. I begged

my mother to let me feed the fox,
but she said no, recalling the obese
black squirrels that circled her

tent when she camped, while pregnant,
in Yosemite. She said
it would follow me

all the rest of my life—why I wanted
to feed the animal
even more. One night I sneaked

a plate of leftover fried chicken wings,
placed it by the back door
and in the morning, no flesh

was left. Nothing except
a paw print browned in old grease,
ghosted to the bone china's edge.

Omens I Chose to Ignore

Our two-bedroom duplex filled with more string basses
than guests. The parched graveyard by the freeway where we
tried to find Lightnin' Hopkins' plot. We did not. Once, I was lying
down on the green couch with medicine you squeezed
from a blue baster fizzing in my ear. But I could hear
our neighbor's drunk uncle as he crashed his truck
into our side of the brick house. We could have been
sitting right there, under the live oak, where we dared to sip
red wine in the humidity, in the shin-high cool of the concrete
porch. I remember the cockroach that slipped into the stemless
glass in the crabgrass by my ankle, how the bug flailed
as it drowned and you said, *At least he'll die happy.* That night,
by accident, I threw my new red corduroy cut-offs
in with the whites and dyed the whole soaking load.

Last Nostalgia Starting with a Piece of Spider Plant on Our Car's Backseat

You moved clippings of your childhood spider plant
with us in a Ziploc half-filled with tap water

so we could grow something once rooted in the cool
valleys of Blacksburg in our new

Houston duplex. You kept a photograph of me—
where I perch on a brick wall in Richmond, by a coal train

idling near the muddy James—tacked to the velvet
insides of your fiddle case, its interior the purple

nap of coffins. I often wonder if you made it
back to your mountain town, if your friend Sheff—

the cokehead gravedigger—is still around, if he does
bumps in his pickup as he waits

for that day's mourners to leave, so he can jump
on the coffin to get it all the way down,

which upsets the family if they linger
and see it. And you used to say *I* was the ghoul,

cutting my baked potato in front of the late
blue light of my true-crime shows. You know,

a woman was once found crouched in her
killer's white mini-fridge. This was

years later: her body rigid, her expression
still perfectly intact.

Past Life Evaporation Riff

The scent of the jasmine comes in heavy
as a past life. Like the one you left

after those years in Houston. You've cracked
the window now so you can sleep
with a breeze. You could never

sleep with the windows open
in Texas, or you'd let

in the swamp by degrees: the muscadine's
clusters of hard violet, the sunflowers
seared bald, socketed to the red

sides of the dried riverbed. Even the armadillos
tongued the cypress knees, foraging

like sleepwalkers. You often feel the swamp's
hot marrow inside you as it grows
here in this dry Southern

California June, as it blooms
through your pillow. You feel the dragged

ghost of its humidity tapping
that code you can't break. Those days
you'd wake, too late in the afternoon,

after daring the last night's weather: you sipped
a heavy red on your front porch

instead of white. When you woke
a steep hangover tunneled,
deep as mirrors. Your sleep, years later,

in the West Coast, still builds shrines
to the stunted relics of Texan magnolias:

those blunt buds
the shriveled hands of martyrs
without a church. They'd thumb your half-

parted lips. What's left
to worship? Not the summer

idling like a white pickup. Not the drunk
who hit the side of your apartment
on Ridgewood, took off with a limp

through the backlit oleanders. Not the oleanders
slick with blood the politicians

call *illegal.* What could you do to sleep
in Houston? You'd get up
from your insomnia,

from your then-lover and walk
the neighborhood at night as automatic

sprinklers chirred and hissed,
slicked your arms. In the dark
evaporation you'd feel your cells

shimmer, your temperature drop
a degree, maybe two. Your body

just cool enough
to wade in, walk through.

TWO

To the Peeping Tom Who Disguised Himself
as an Oklahoma Night

You'd have to morph into a California
twilight to find me here, to stare

through my bathroom's cracked window
as you wear your scuba diver's wet suit, your black

nylon mask with two slashed eye-slits. It's late,
and I don't know why I watch these true-

crime shows alone, my husband out of town
for the weekend. To release the steam

after my shower, I have to hand-crank the window
open a few inches, which is

the exact opportunity you confess
you look for: no venetian blinds, that one

lit window throwing a woman's nude
form onto your personal porno screen. It seems

you've already been caught, though I can't stop
imagining your camouflage

midnighting the gap in my cracked
bathroom window. No ventilation fan. And

although the glass opens onto my neighbor's bamboo,
even you, in your potbelly, could probably

shimmy between the houses. But you'd make
a lousy California night—your eye-slits

silver and hollow as grain silos, your round,
midwestern face: graceless and landlocked. I always

sleep with the front door triple-
bolted when I'm the only one around. I hold

conversations with the cat. I dance
with my unfogging body doubled

in the mirrored medicine cabinet—the window
thrown open to the night. I know if you broke

out of prison, hitchhiked here, and slipped
through the bamboo for a glimpse,

I'd recognize you. The wet air, the window
open to the ocean's salt. You walk wearing

a different darkness than mine, that whole
parched region on your back.

Asymmetrical—

Mole on my shoulder. Road map
of the whole damn state
of Texas. His left arm—darker
and more freckled than the other
from dangling it out the window
of his pickup while driving. That dream
where I grind down the top
row of my bleached teeth. I broke
our lease after three and a half years. That dream
where I'm bitten by something large
and swift underwater. Crawfish
in a pile at the seafood diner—live—all
waiting to one side of the tank.

Reasons Why Licking the Anesthetic Backs of Waxy Monkey Tree Frogs Could've Made Me Stand Living in Texas

Because it's what trainers gave their horses
in order to suppress the feel of injuries because

the potion's forty times stronger than morphine
because in a Texas heat my breath

on the pillow is the equator because insomnia
the hottest spot throbs in both ears

because three and a half years is too long to live
in a place where that bar commissioned

a statue on its patio of a car-sized
armadillo with a mirrored shell

because when I drove past the creature each day
on my way to school my reflection broke

into well over a hundred
pieces because this was

the price the swamp required
because I felt every part of my body move farther

and farther off like a galaxy
even if I looked away

In the Categories of Smells, Pears Are Considered Ethereal

Where are you? isn't a question
I can ask his pears,

their dropped yellows softening
the facets of the black
humpbacked flies

which swarm, hip-high,
over the orchard's floor. He's dead

a decade now, leaving no one
in Greenwood, Mississippi, who still shares
our blood,

save one: my aunt in the wheat-colored
doublewide next door to her father's

fester of pears. Before he died
she used to change
his adult diaper while he watched

TV. And each time
she'd announce loudly

that he'd wet himself. The last time
I visited, at nineteen, I walked with him
through the ruined pear trees—too sweet

and too late to save—though they
weren't like him at all.

I didn't go to the funeral.
Two months before, I'd lied
to my art history professor,

said my grandfather had died. I was the curve
for the exam I took early so I could make

the concert in time. I couldn't go
to the real service because I'd used up
the excuse. But I could imagine

the scent of his fruit trees in fall
might slip through my aunt's

trailer as a ghost
woven from the golden night-
fiber of old pears

and move past
the plaster garden gnomes she hoards, past

her twenty-pound grey cat, past
the last woman who remains
there in the bloodline

if she dares to leave
even one window cracked.

Nocturnal Activity

Last night I knocked
the tip off my right canine
while grinding my teeth. The sound:
an animal scavenging
through gravel. Have you
(former lover, Virginia
blues bassist) left me
with this habit I can't break? The way
I'd grind through the night
those seven years and you—heavy
sleeper—would never
notice or wake. Today
I walk from room
to room and massage the knots
on either side of my jaw, a soreness
under each earlobe dull
as a matte hubcap, a scratched
mirror. What's worse
than grinding down your own
bones as a habit? Meet me at
the old lepers' hospital we once
stumbled on just past Baton
Rouge and bring
your blues, and I'll bring
all of the teeth I have
left to lose.

Mississippi: Origins

My parents come from a place where all the houses stop
at one story

for the heat. Where every porch—front
and back—simmers in black screens that sieve

mosquitoes from our blood. Where everyone knows
there's only one kind of tea:

sweet. The first time my father
introduced my mother to his parents,

his mother made my mother change
the bed sheets in the guest room. She'd believed it

a gesture of intimacy. My grandmother
saved lavender hotel soaps and lotions

to wrap and mail as gifts at Christmas. My grandfather
once shot the head off a rattlesnake

in the gravel driveway of the house he built
in Greenwood. He gave the dry rattle to my mother

the same week I was born, saying, *Why don't you
make something out of it.*

Blues for the Semiaquatic

Each time I feed the green lake
my stale apricot granola, it offers only
a pack of rat-tailed nutria

in return. They swim toward me,
their bucktooth incisors stained
from their body's own iron—those bright red

front teeth. I know a thing or two
about mutiny, how a wound can
conform to any shape. You often say,

I moved here for you, as you slam
your door and splinter a few
low notes on the cello. I go

to the public park where people waver
through trails as they hold black
umbrellas in the heat. No rain. When you

gave up wheat, we thought
the stomach pains would stop, but the aches
came sharp and straight

from the landscape. Look at the Ouzo
you bought—finally, a liquor free
of barley. One shot clouds your tumbler

of water white. Watch the swamprats
I've summoned draw closer, slowly
rusting from something inside.

I Have a Problem with the Erotic History of Musk

Those red, jellied secretions from the guts
of East Asian deer

make the base notes in many
perfumes labeled *musk*. What I learned next

shivered from a scent
to a bleat as I read that ancient

shepherds first discovered the scent
of musk from sheep-fucking,

from the pungent fragrance
released by the animals'

anal glands. And this
is a problem for me. This

bothers me, even though the vials
of musk in my medicine

cabinet were brewed
from synthetic recipes. I don't want

even these bruised
approximations or the way

a dab of musk under each
pulsing earlobe calls near

a cornered or kicking animal,
a cry. What did you say

last night when you
bent near my ear? What

were you coming here for
if not to dissolve

one time into another, this
brick house into a Bronze

Age field. The scent of
that body—ancient—as it yields.

Victorian Chamber Pot My Mother Used as a Planter for Climbing Ivy

Why I'd imagine phantom asses
floating over the television as a child:
that cast porcelain bowl sat on top

of the TV in the den for decades—
its fat ivory base, flared lip, and ear-
shaped handle. It looked

like a giant white teacup spilling
devil's ivy up the walls. The vine climbed
all the way to the ceiling's corner

before doubling back to the carpet. Before
I was born, my mother bought
the chamber pot for five bucks

at a flea market near Ottawa. At a cocktail
party that night she told a doctor
she was thinking of using it

as a soup tureen and he gagged
on his brandy, said the uric
acid could still be lodged

in the pot's hairline cracks. So, no gumbo
ever simmered in the antique
piss of Victorians, no molecular secret

fumed from my lips or escaped
the flawed glaze. I once waitressed
at a café in Richmond

which served its buffet brunch
from a claw-foot bathtub
the owner had found in an alley

and enthroned on a long table
in the center of the restaurant. He hung
the plexiglass sneeze guard on brass chains

over its mouth like a budget
chandelier. Each Sunday, I'd fill the tub
with ice cubes, line the hump with raw kale,

place bowls of lox, rye toast, scrambled
eggs, and cantaloupe in the kinked
green foliage. After church

rouged ladies would scoop
breakfast from the bathtub
onto their plates with metal tongs

while I brewed coffee and pictured
the naked genitals of bathers rising
wet from the porcelain,

shivered and blue-tipped
from the ice. Halfway through
my shift the lox would disappear, leaving

its bowl slick. A pink strip of it always
caught on the tub's edge, bent,
almost raised, like a finger.

Swan Fingers

Each time the scent of fried pork rinds eclipsed

her gardenias, my grandmother knew
it must be her charred

elbow burning
as she leaned its numb tip
on the still-

hot eye of her stove. Her disease
of the connective tissue meant

she couldn't process collagen
properly, meant blocked
nerves and arms

bruised and barbed

with white scarwork. As a child my mother
liked to squeeze

her mother's spongy hands, wiggle
her loose joints, tug the iguana-flap

on her neck that would stretch

and snap like elastic. Once
when my grandmother had her teeth
cleaned as a girl, the dentist

nicked her gums with a steel pick and the hairline cut
gushed blood down her neck. He kept

stuffing her mouth with cotton, but the wound
wouldn't clot so he finally phoned
for an ambulance. He tipped her head

farther back. In old age, she'd stroke
her own throat as a habit, fold

her hands in her lap as if to hide
their misaligned joints, her fingers
crooked and kinked

due to "swan neck deformity." As a kid
I'd beg to pet the curved
necks of her "birds," so she'd hold
out her palms and wiggle

her digits. Her disease—
Ehlers-Danlos—would dissolve

eight feet of her intestines with gangrene, would take
both of her lungs, would repeatedly collapse
her rectum. Her brother

had it, her mother and father, her youngest
daughter. My mother's the first

person on that side
of the family—the Swedish Bleeders—

not to receive it, although she,
my sister, and I can bend
our thumb-tips to our wrists, pivot

our double-jointed necks
around like owls. My mother's skin's

so sensitive she can write on it—raise a red

cursive on her body with a dragged hangnail. But we don't
bruise or bleed as easily
as my grandmother. I was five

and didn't know the real name for it or why
her blue-tubed

tank of oxygen hissed. Her skin
too loose and too soft. I thought

all grandmothers must be textured
like this. I called her

bent fingers: "swans."

I Find a Photograph Online of a Taxidermied Fox
Posed in Front of a Flaming Grey Paisley Couch
Abandoned in a Field of Crabgrass

—*after the photograph* Fox, 2004, *by Jody Fausett*

If this were a fable of insomnia, the cloth
couch on fire would be mine—
pea green—and the dead

fox, its right foot raised,
would be a waifish
Texan coyote. Don't tell me

to brew chamomile tea
for a proper remedy. What I've
got is humidity

hot as marrow
working its slow way through
the blue paint in my bathroom,

sponging the windows' seals
slick and loose
as honeysuckle. I fight

the new urge to write
the photographer from Dawsonville,
Georgia, to ask if he too

sits up late on a concrete porch
sipping something with fizz. Night
like a wick. I want to see if

he'll drive to Houston soon
with a gas can and a red fox
frozen in an arsonist's

pose. To see if he knows
how long a night
burns once we light it.

THREE

One Year after My Move to California, I Jell-O Wrestle My Texan Past in a Dream

You visit me with your pockets filled with swamp water, the sunflowers
husked and unshaved—an anniversary bouquet
of faces which rise, with you and the temperature,

to strangers. I don't want to know
whose names now fold
into our old mailbox on Ridgewood. I could

only walk the neighborhood at night
when the heat sank to the eighties. I could almost
love the stubbled javelinas for charging us once

as we stayed too late at the alligator preserve. We must've
turned to a stand of live oaks in the twilight,
startled the blind herd as we breathed. In the dream

you hold a steel bowl of green Jell-O, ask if I remember
the roadhouse off I-59. The one that advertised women in bikinis
who'd slide into a rink to wrestle each other smeared

in gelatin. I told you—as we drove by the bar—which ghosts
Jell-O holds in its shiver: pig skin, ground bones, bovine hide.
I'd slick myself down to a glimmer

here in the space of this dream,
where the blades of the date palms serrate and slit the sky
so I might escape. So I'd glow green

in my second skin. I'd slip from the rink's
loose ropes, from my marrow-scrubbed double in the bikini
who now shrinks to a crouch, from my past and its

ground-up dead, which I've simmered and stirred all year
to arrive here: their faces sealed as they fade
to translucence, smooth and finally cooled.

My Grandparents' Siamese Cat, Sheba, Brain Damaged from a Crochet Hook

She'd been pawing a loop of crochet come loose
at the yellow edge of the half-finished baby afghan

as my grandmother got up to pull the peach shortbread
from the oven. One aluminum hook rolled off

the kitchen table and shot into Sheba's right seal-point ear,
stabbing her frontal lobe like a javelin. Joelle,

a patient of my grandfather's in the psych ward,
was a former child beauty queen from Hot Coffee,

Mississippi. Her father owned a café named
for the town and had banned cream and sugar. He believed

they weakened the flavor of his roasted beans'
gamey hazelnut. The day after he caught Joelle kissing

his head waitress at sixteen, he drove his daughter
to Jackson for the lobotomy. Since then she'd rocked

into her thirties without speaking until my grandfather
lowered the dosage of her sedatives. He'd refused

to perform electroshock or lobotomies,
called the shrinks who fried and sliced people

butchers and quacks. Joelle finally spoke one word:
molasses—the only condiment her father

ever dropped into his own coffee. My grandfather
drove his injured cat to the vet to euthanize her.

When the technician raised the syringe, he grabbed
her wrist and asked if he didn't put Sheba to sleep,

would she be in pain for the rest of her life? The vet said
she'd never walk straight from the brain damage

but her puncture would heal. My grandfather took
Sheba home—alive—where she learned to lean

against walls for balance. He left cushions propped up
like a fence from their bedroom to the kitchen. Each night

Sheba shuffled across the house to eat, bounced
from spongy pillow to pillow. She'd always return, purring,

to the bedside where my grandfather, half-asleep,
would turn. He'd reach down into the dark and lift her up.

Middle School Sleepover: Jessica Accidentally Steps on My Right Eye

When her dry hangnail scraped the white
surface of my eye, I was thirteen, too
mortified to scream. In history class

I was too shy to tug up my strapless
bra as it sagged around my waist and made
with my real breasts above it

a bumpy udder. I nudged
the loose cups with my elbows under
the stares of wigged presidents

on posters, hoping
no one would notice. The night
of the sleepover, Jessica rose to pee. She could

only half-see in the blackness,
stumbled her way back to the den,
through six of us sprawled

in sleeping bags on the floor. My spine
sharp over hardwood. I'd been lying
awake for hours when her big toe

poked my open eye in the dark. I flipped
onto my side, coughed twice.
In the morning my right eye

was wholly bloodshot, crusted and
half-closed. Jessica's mom
worried that I'd give

all of the other girls pink eye.
She handed me a patch from their garage's
stash of Halloween costumes,

said, *Wear this, honey. Lady,*
your daughter's a bigfoot, I thought
but didn't say, waving to Jessica

as I stepped from her porch, crossed
the street in front of a blinking
red stoplight. My eye

pulsed as the girls backed away
and I turned, snapping the black
strap of my pirate's patch.

Trompe-l'oeil for Shannon

The punk chick who used to cut
my hair at her salon near the railroad

tracks in Austin had a black
bob with a blue streak, a half-inch

tattoo of a bug inked to the tip
of her right elbow—that ribbed, grey

oval of a roly-poly. As a kid
Shannon would flip rotten dogwood

logs with her sister to expose
whole writhing colonies. She'd nudge

the pill bugs with a soft finger
so they'd hunch in their armored shells,

ball themselves into the smallest
armadillos. This was before

the divorce. Before their mother packed them
in the tan Buick at midnight to drive

farther south. Their albino
bull terrier's pink-gummed grin

quivered in the front seat. Each time
their parents shouted she'd slip

from the house, take her little sister
to the rotten logs to play

with the pill bugs. That day she spun me
in the leather swivel chair, stopped it

so I could stare at her elbow, nose-
level with her tattoo. She wanted to

show me its secret. She bent her arm
slowly so the roly-poly

stretched over the bump of her joint. As she
straightened her arm, her elbow-

skin puckered and pulled
the antennae back. The bug shrank

to a silver stud where—armored
and compact—no one, Shannon said,

her steel shears in hand, no one would
ever dare fuck with it.

I Sip an Herbal Tea Called *Gypsy Cold Care*

Today, I could brine
the backyard's dropped olives
with my watery stare. Don't ask me

to do my taxes. Don't ask me the capital
of Tanzania or any eastern
bra-shaped state. Leave

my brain out of this. Today,
the silver-dollar eucalyptus offers
to pay all my debts

then signs the air
in invisible ink. The air's pores
clogged with menthol. And the rose hips

and cinnamon kick up
through the licorice root
brewed with my herbal tea. I'd like to believe

in the recipe, in the gypsy
who once crushed cloves
in peppermint, hyssop

in yarrow. My mother keeps
a framed photograph of a French gypsy—
our ancestor who wears

my mother's dark hair
with its blunt white part and the plum-
colored mole on her chin's

left side. I whisper *Saraliza*
and sip. This is all
I can manage with a head cold. This is

the old ghost leaving
her herbs behind as she steps
into the boat, as she marries

her sailor at sea,
as she leans on the ship's white edge
with the scrawled recipe

she once stuffed in a bottle. She shivers,
lets it drop. Over a hundred
years later I swallow.

Blue Honey

When I read that French bees
had sipped the sugared waste

that dripped from an M&M's factory,
carrying the candy-liquid back

to their hives, and stoppered
the round cells with blue honey,

I knew you must still be
thinking of me. Why else

would the honeycombs clot
their golds and blues in layers to shape

those exact shades of the stained-glass
sky in that Baptist church's window

that overlooked our former street
in Texas? The bells

wouldn't let us sleep in
on Sundays, which was

my punishment from the swamp
each time I cursed

its heat. Like me
the bees don't speak

French, though they'd recognize
the uvular *r*'s of my old

Cajun neighbors in the whirr
of their wings. Like me

they keep going back
to a crack in the stained glass,

to the factory. They keep
moving toward sweetness, they

keep carrying the weight of
that deepest blue.

Accidental Theft: Crazy Quilt

What should I do with your ancestors'
dresses? Their old calicos sewn in patternless

blotches like the Texan heat. When we
split, I packed your crazy quilt

by accident as I boxed up
my half of the house. You took

all of the spatulas, left our stemless
wineglasses still fused with faint coral

prints of my lower lip. I'd ship
the quilt to your new address

if I had it, if only to quiet the dead
whose fabric holds

roses from a hundred years ago, so maybe
their skirts will stop rustling

as I turn in the sheets. But maybe
you've left me

this quilt on purpose so I'll never
get to sleep, so I'll simmer under the heat

of your blood in its twisted
generations. Maybe those jagged patches

of violet, red velvet, and calico,
like scar tissue exposed,

will flush in sun, deepen
each time I turn on the light.

Visiting Richmond after Several Years Away, I Discover a Restaurant Called L'Opossum

—for Mary Flinn

When possums age their ears loosen and drop
off, my friend Mary tells me

over dinner. Their tails, too. I spear another
oiled lobe of squid on my plate. Late April hovers

on the cusp of summer, nearly slipping
midroutine, like a ventriloquist. I mention

my hoarder aunt, Becky, who wears
an extra-large Marsupial Rescue League of Texas

T-shirt, keeps a pet possum named Georgia
sleeping beneath the china cabinet with her three

snaggletoothed babies. There are ways to return
to a city like a cat steps through the glass

knickknacks displayed on a fireplace's mantle
without wrecking anything. This

isn't one of them. The storefronts
have changed their faces. Someone hogs

my favorite iron bench woven with rosettes
in the cemetery that overlooks a coal train

smoking on its tracks. I can't tell
if the white blinds in my old row house now

rented by another couple once belonged
to me or just happen to be

bent in the identical corner by a new
indoor cat. Nothing is exactly

the same as I left it.
Except the river. The slow wisteria

thickens its gnarled ankles
in the cobblestone alleys that conjure

the Civil War. Mary says the ancient
bones of possums go back

to the dinosaurs, that they step
among us, prehensile, only-half

dissolved. There's a grey ear lost
to the potted hydrangea. And the restaurant

with the mock-French name
heats with the chatter of diners, knives

dragged across plates. I'm glad
we came here, I tell her. The place that used to be

my favorite café is now painted
cornflower blue and hung

with framed portraits of the oldest, most
adaptable animal—black eyes,

a knack for fainting, a high
tolerance for rattlesnake poison. I push out

my chair and rise to walk
to the bathroom. I know it's still there

at the end of the hallway. Its mirror
with the chin-level L-

shaped scar now wears a frame
of scalloped brass. It holds the traffic

stopped around Stonewall's statue,
the shabby mimosas

fattening by the path. It holds
those freckles broken over my shoulder—

so much more than it's ever
going to give back.

Welcome, Stranger

said the letters in buttercream cursive on top of the baby-
shower's cake in braided pink and blue icing

because no one knew
if I'd be born
a girl or boy. In the same photograph of the party,
my mother hunches

on the couch in a sack-like jeans-jumper,
hands folded on top of her pregnant belly. She looks
sideways at the cake. The night before

she dreamed she gave birth
to a blind and squeaking grey tabby. *I was surprised,*
she tells me, years later,
but I decided to love it anyway. She cradled the kitten

against her bare breast and began
to nurse it. I say a kitten
would've been easier to handle than me

at fifteen—the pink hair, the junkie lover,
the friend who scrawled three upside-down
crosses on the forehead

of my sister's battery-powered doll:
Baby Secrets. They shaved

her scalp, too. *Can I tell you a secret?*
it whispered. *I love you.* My father once

spotted me walking to school
as he cruised past in the backseat of his carpool, as the driver
snorted, *Good lord, glad that's
not my daughter,* and my dad said,

That's my daughter. In the old photograph
he raises his pint glass for a toast and grasps
the tip of his ivory

cigarette holder. One guest's about to slap his back,

but the hand hangs there,
mid-air. The impact
hasn't yet hit him.

Reminder to My Past Self in Which I Employ the Scientific Term *Drunken Forest*

It's like that time I blew a hole
through my right eardrum while scuba diving. Sixteen
years old. Seventeen

miles off the Texas coast, I got stuck just
twenty feet below the ocean's surface—couldn't clear
my ears because of a head cold. I've been reading

all morning about the polar ice caps, how the frost
that covers an Alaskan lake now melts
and bubbles with methane released

from ancient carbon. The decaying plants haven't
seen sunlight in 30,000 years, but they've begun
to thaw; and in the past, which holds

my younger self underwater, my head nods
and turns from side to side to release
the pressure. As the rise in temperatures sizzles

frost into lakes, the black spruces slump and cross
into a *drunken forest.* I discover photographs
of the leaning trees in the *New York Times,*

the fractured Alaskan lake. I imagine my old
selves crossing, slumping, as my uncle leans
along the rail of the top deck of the dive boat.

He'd coached me: ask the dreadlocked scuba instructor
where we can buy a bag of weed. My pilot
uncle with the weak ventricle who couldn't pass

his last health exam and so could no longer fly,
who got us certified for diving. As I tried
to rise toward the water's surface, I heard a whistle

as my right eardrum split, as bubbles poured
from the rip, as I waited, as I pulsed
in the middle of the sound. I imagine the sound

of the ice as it breaks, now in the north,
is the same note I once heard as I rose
to crack the Gulf Coast's surface, vertigo shaking

the boat, the hands of my uncle as he tugged me
up the ladder. Later, I found my pillowcase pocked
with wisps of blood—the dark spider-marks on cotton

twisted like spruce roots. Two more nights
on the dive boat without antibiotics, I felt my ear fester
and fill like a lake. Though I couldn't hear

from my right ear for months, in my nightmares there was
that terrible whistle that could split whole landscapes,
could dizzy and drown a forest. I'd wake

from the sound to find my bed in the bottom
cabin of the boat still shaking. A kind of quiet so thin
one sucked-in breath—let out—could break it.

FOUR

The Atheist Wore Goat Silk

I've wanted to visit the genetically modified goat
spliced with silkworm DNA
spinning white threads from its pink udders
like a piebald spider. I've wondered how much
for a whole goat silk dress? I always save
the spiders that shimmy near my eyes
but never the bristled silverfish
which drop to the boatwood dinner table
from the skylight. Come Indian Summer
the fuchsia bougainvillea unpurses
its dry lips, licks the sweat
from my neck. My mother tells her childhood
best friend—who's dying from liver
cancer in Jackson, who consults
a Pentecostal woman who speaks
in tongues—that her two daughters
are atheists. Meaning my little sister and me.
Somewhere there's a goat that squirts
a rare silk so bizarre maybe
no one would actually wear it. That webbed dress
sticking to my chest, the grandfather
clock, all over the bedroom walls like a past
that drags everything with it. The thread
leading back to an animal I badly
need to believe in. Its impossible milk
steams in the twilight. There's a dress
that rises from its udders with a misted
sleeve I can almost see.

Summer of Choosing the Dress

There can't be a right one
for this occasion. Not racy
chiffon, not crepe, not plain

cotton. My mother's best
friend, Donna, is dying. Her liver
has mutinied, has begun

to throw her overboard. Soon
she must choose a pattern, a color,
a cut. Once, I watched

my lover's roommate—a soldier
back from Iraq—leap screaming
from a couch to buzz

a bald stripe down the orange
spine of an alley cat
that had peed on his pillowcase. He

switched off the electric
razor, asked me, if I had to choose
fire or drowning, which

would be the best
way to go. I said probably
water. He said, *No.*

Too slow. I don't know why
he kept squirrel meat stacked
in the freezer next to the bags

of snow peas as if they belonged
together. I don't know what to do
except mark the weeks

by her chemo, wonder which
dress she'll pick. There isn't a best
choice, so I'll keep

her options open. Black cocktail
or a peach neckline low
as her alto. Calico climbing

her chest, her liver, entwined
as if all those
twisted roses could hold.

Fried Chicken Prom Corsage (2): *Danse Macabre*

There are inventions, like that bouquet of fried chicken
winging a girl's wrist, the kind

you wouldn't have believed existed. Bird
in the hand. In the teeth. A late-night treat

for the drunk munchies. You want to see the photographs
snapped after midnight when the blond prom dates gnaw

their pink-ribboned corsages to the gristle. And there's the yellow
hardcover housed in a college library

bound in human skin. You glimpsed its wide pores
butterflied in yesterday's newspaper. *A book about the human soul*

deserved to have a human covering, says
the text's inscription. Once, you skipped the high

school prom, dropped acid under a wild
dogwood instead. You've read that the woman

whose hide was stretched for the book was mentally
ill and died of a heart attack. You've looked up

the twisted florist in Kentucky who sells the tufted
fried chicken corsage. Maybe she's trying to resurrect

an old tradition. Several times, you've considered packing
your black lace, making the drive.

Our Weeklong Stay in the Magnolia Hotel that Started with a Mermaid Skeleton: Hurricane Evacuation, Austin

The night I heard the mermaid skeleton dug up
from the Black Sea was a hoax, we toasted her photograph

on TV anyway, opened all the one-shot
vodkas from our room's mini-fridge. You refused to feel

guilty that the hurricane gave us a vacation, a reason
to flee the swamp for hill country. Once I got used to rhubarb

jelly on rye in the mornings, canoeing through the afternoons,
the way that movie theater had the slimmest maple tabletops

installed in front of the seats for drinks, I said,
This could be our lives: 160 miles west and far

better. You bought me a necklace crocheted with freshwater
pearls from a stand at the farmers' market. Years later I tossed it

into the garbage after we split. The tip of your right pinky's
fingernail always greyer than the others from the way

you'd twist and tamp down the ash. In the dim
room I smoothed the amber bedspread—

pattered in hydrangeas—the clusters that covered every
rip and stain. When the photographer dragged the fleshless

tail of a barracuda to shore and glued it to the torso
of human medical skeleton, the bones—for a moment—

looked whole. As they sat in the sand we agreed
that they looked almost perfectly matched.

Last Barbecue

My grandfather's lover, Bob, brought a box of white chocolate-
covered fire ants to the barbecue. Their wives watched
from the picnic table as my grandfather dropped a treat
onto each child's stuck-out tongue: my mother's, my aunt's,
and Jack's—Bob and Mary Lou's six-year-old son. *Those kids
sure are brave,* my grandmother said, tossing paper plates
across the blue checkered tablecloth, before Jack shrieked,
You said they were raisins! and ran inside. The screen door banged
in time to Bob slapping my grandfather's back. Mary Lou
rose and said her eyes watered from the propane
mosquito fogger. The steam had just changed directions
as my grandmother covered her lips with the rim of a plate.

Biosentimentality

—*The emotional complications that arise after one person's tissue is sutured into another's. Patients will often imagine a relationship to their tissue donors.*

When the black lab chewed off my nose
and hard palate, I'd passed

out from the pinot
noir and white

handful of Ambien. And when

I finally reached for my cigarettes, one slipped
from the hole

where my lips had vanished. He must've
been hungry. I must've been

unconscious on the bath mat
all week without waking. When the surgeons

sewed a dead woman's nose, lips, and chin

to my skull, I didn't ask
her name or where

she was from, but the papers

printed it: a middle-
aged suicide who'd hanged herself in her French

village just days
before the operation. And when I began

to regain the taste
of a tangerine's meat, the whiff of menthol

from a stale pack, I could feel her

senses still pulsing. I repainted
my bathroom from a bucket

of French blue, hung a thrift-store

portrait of a cottage near the window. I got
strong men to tear

out the tub and replace it
with a claw-foot. I put

a provincial armoire in the corner. Once, I dropped
my robe to the carpet and caught myself

nude in the mirror—the frame always
tilted slightly back.

I had to stop

staring at my neck. When my right hand
moved to unhook

my rose gold chain, I felt myself
tug just once, and the skin

under my chin rippled. That's when I tore
each swinging curtain

in the house from its rod, each loose
lace tie, I removed

every possible noose.

Rapture

So his Baptist parents and Jesus wouldn't see,
my old boyfriend kept his heavy metal

CDs inside plastic Kenny Rogers
jewel cases in high school. His father, finding

his stash of jerk-off socks, said masturbation
would make him grow up wanting

the bodies of men. He told me
his mother once disappeared

as she turned the corner of a pile of white
corn stacked at their grocery store. He believed

the Rapture had happened, had left him, eight
years old, alone to wander the hairy red walls

of display sweet potatoes as their slow eyes
began to slide toward the floor—the tubers

soft and rotted. I haven't thought
of Ed in a while, though the Internet tells me

his new girlfriend goes by the nickname
Drain Bamaged, has long red hair. Long after

we broke up he served a year inside Richmond City
for selling pot, where he lived in a barred pen

with a blaring TV and twenty other men, his shoes
tucked under his pillow as he slept. I'd mail him

letters and the books about cults he'd requested
and visit every few months. The last time

I sat in the see-through booth we spoke
but couldn't hug or touch due

to the plastic partition. I said, before leaving,
Imaginary tequila shot! and we each raised

an invisible glass. We laughed
as we clinked them, threw our heads back.

Eat Shit, Martine: Prescription for a
Southern Belle

Because my southern mother never cussed
growing up, didn't learn

the meaning of the word *turd*
until she turned twenty,

her college roommate from Montgomery,
Martine, made her say each day

instead of *Good morning:*
Eat shit, Martine. If my mother spoke

other words before the prescribed
greeting, Martine crossed her arms

and cleared her throat as a prompt: *Well?*
It's a lovely day, my mother said,

rising in her white nightgown
from the twin bed, *a lovely day*

to eat shit, Martine! Each day for a year
she said it so when her professor

told her she should stop wasting time
and make babies or when her first lover

decided not to propose, she was ready
to unleash the proper response: *Eat shit,*

Professor. Eat shit, Jim. Shibboleth
for a new life, a blue tongue.

As a Child, My Mother Took a Girl Scout Field Trip to the Men's Ward of a New Orleans Prison

When she told me the prisoners stood by—polite,
no catcalls, mostly black—as she followed the other

ten-year-old white girls down the dark aisle that divided
the men's barred cells, I asked which Girl Scout

badge, exactly, were they earning? Mass
Incarceration, White Privilege, Voyeurism? Although I'd quit

my own troop by fourth grade (reasons: mean girls,
forced diaper changing, infrequent camping), I'd saved

my old SWAP hat as a memento—that maroon baseball cap
safety-pinned with the fuzzy crafts we'd made

to trade with strangers at SWAP meets: a cotton-ball koala
snug in its walnut-shell crib, a clothespin grasshopper

with green pipe-cleaner legs, a miniature felt fried egg
and bacon strip glued to a black bottle cap. I asked my mother

if she remembers which prison, which crepe myrtle-
draped street in 1950s New Orleans, but when we scroll

through the names of jails on the Internet we find
too many to be sure. She remembers some men moved

toward the front of their cells to nod or smile. One said hello.
She remembers reaching to unpin a SWAP to give him,

but her troop leader said no. She remembers the Louisiana heat
moved through everything and she just kept walking.

A Wayward Cow's Worst Nightmare

—headline from the New York Times *regarding the Devil's Rope
Museum, in Texas, dedicated to the history of barbed wire*

It's a wayward cow I now find
in the dream where I'm back in Texas

years after my move to California. It's a wayward
cow—brown with one eye slightly

larger and darker than the other. Wilder, like sides
of a bed in which one

of the two sleepers stays awake
hours later than the other, who turns

in her insomnia to the thin light
that thieves through the door, or

to the cicadas which empty
their loose change into the old

days in their copper stacks. I'm back
in Texas, where a cow

now leads me through
the front door

of the museum. Lengths of barbed wire
stud the walls, budding

their silver oleanders. Don't look, the cow
says with her wilder eye,

don't look at the walls where the wire's
snagged our hide, where our

torn skin, without wind,
sways like paper—it's a wayward

cow I now follow out the door.
I try not to look

as we leave, but I do, once,
and see a woman. She sleepwalks

through the museum in her swamp-
colored dress, her red hair

tangled like the year, like three
and a half—her arms

darken, her scarred
back still mapped.

CPSIA information can be obtained
at www.ICGtesting.com
Printed in the USA
LVOW11s1619150117

521020LV00001B/25/P

9 780807 165683